ISBN 978-0-259-48227-7
PIBN 10819138

This book is a reproduction of an important historical work. Forgotten Books uses state-of-the-art technology to digitally reconstruct the work, preserving the original format whilst repairing imperfections present in the aged copy. In rare cases, an imperfection in the original, such as a blemish or missing page, may be replicated in our edition. We do, however, repair the vast majority of imperfections successfully; any imperfections that remain are intentionally left to preserve the state of such historical works.

1 MONTH OF
FREE
READING

at

www.ForgottenBooks.com

By purchasing this book you are eligible for one month membership to ForgottenBooks.com, giving you unlimited access to our entire collection of over 1,000,000 titles via our web site and mobile apps.

To claim your free month visit: www.forgottenbooks.com/free819138

English
Français
Deutsche
Italiano
Español
Português

www.forgottenbooks.com

Mythology Photography **Fiction**
Fishing Christianity **Art** Cooking
Essays Buddhism Freemasonry
Medicine **Biology** Music **Ancient
Egypt** Evolution Carpentry Physics
Dance Geology **Mathematics** Fitness
Shakespeare **Folklore** Yoga Marketing
Confidence Immortality Biographies
Poetry **Psychology** Witchcraft
Electronics Chemistry History **Law**
Accounting **Philosophy** Anthropology
Alchemy Drama Quantum Mechanics
Atheism Sexual Health **Ancient History**
Entrepreneurship Languages Sport
Paleontology Needlework Islam
Metaphysics Investment Archaeology
Parenting Statistics Criminology
Motivational

DISCOURSE

DELIVERED

HE TRUSTEES, FACULTY, AND ST

OF

RUTGERS COLLEGE,

AT

EW-BRUNSWICK, NEW-JERSEY

ON

THE 14TH OF JULY, 1829, THE DAY PRECE

ANNUAL COMMENCEMENT

BY JOHN SERGEANT, L L. D.

RARY MEMBER OF THE PHILOCLEAN SOC

DISCOURSE

DELIVERED

BEFORE THE TRUSTEES, FACULTY, AND STUDENTS

OF

RUTGERS COLLEGE,

AT

NEW-BRUNSWICK, NEW-JERSEY,

ON

TUESDAY, THE 14TH OF JULY, 1829, THE DAY PRECEDING THE
ANNUAL COMMENCEMENT

BY JOHN SERGEANT, L L. D.

HONORARY MEMBER OF THE PHILOCLEAN SOCIETY.

PUBLISHED AT THE REQUEST OF THE PHILOCLEAN
SOCIETY.

RUTGERS PRESS.

PRINTED FOR THE SOCIETY BY TERHUNE & LETSON.

::*:::::::::::::::::::::::

1829.

Extract from the Minutes of the Philoclean Society, July 14th, 1829.

Resolved, That the thanks of the Philoclean Society be given to the Hon. JOHN SERGEANT, for the learned and impressive Address delivered by him, at their request—and that a copy thereof be solicited for publication.

GARRET I. GARRETSON,
GEORGE A. VROOM,
Committee to inform Mr. Sergeant of the above Resolution.

DISCOURSE.

Gentlemen of the Philoclean and Peithessophian Societies!

THE occasion which has brought us together is calculated to awaken earnest and anxious reflection. Youth is the season of preparation for manhood. In a short time, those who are in a course of training for the duties of life, will, in the order of Providence, succeed to the charge which is now borne by their seniors; and distributed among the varied employments of social and civilized existence, be called by their own strength, each in his allotted sphere, to sustain, preserve, and improve the advantages which are derived to them from their predecessors. To fit them for the task which is thus to devolve upon them, is the design of all education.

In what manner, and by what means this great design may be most effectually accomplished—what are the methods most likely to aid in forming a wise and virtuous man, an honest and useful citizen, is a question of great interest, which cannot be too deeply pondered. An eminent man of antiquity has remarked, with equal beauty and force, that "a state without youth, would be like a year without the Spring." But what avails the Spring, if its blossoms perish without producing fruit or seed? If sporting for a while in the gaiety of the season, and charming the senses with their bloom and fragrance, they disappoint the hope which forms their greatest value, and dwindle, fade and die, as if they had never been?

The insect obeys the law of its ephemeral existence; it spreads its wings in the sunshine, rejoices in a moment of life, and then flutters and disappears. The brute animal is governed by its appetites, and guided by its instinct. It is neither acquainted with its faculties, nor capable of improving them. The individual and the species, for successive generations, move on in their appointed course, without undergoing any sensible change, as little subject to degeneracy from any neglect or folly of their own, as they are able, by their own efforts, to exalt or improve their nature. They live, and they die—they sink into inanimate matter, and are lost in the uninformed mass.

But man is endowed by his Maker with moral and intellectual powers, which not only distinguish him from all the visible creation, but absolutely separate him from any affinity with it. His bodily frame is dust, fearfully and wonderfully made; but still a portion of inanimate matter, which cleaves to the ground! His bodily powers, his sensual passions and appetites have their dwelling upon the earth, in common with the animal creation. His intellect—his power of "large discourse, looking before and after,"—aspires to communion with intelligence, and seeks its kindred beyond the limits of this life. His animal nature may truly say to the worm, " Thou art my brother, and to corruption, Thou art my sister and my mother!" His intellectual and moral faculties have no fellowship upon earth.

These faculties are the talent which his Maker has given to man. By means of them, he is enabled to exercise dominion over the earth, and to subdue it to his own enjoyment and happiness. By their means too, it is intended that he shall exercise dominion over the earthly parts of himself—that he shall regulate the exercise of his corporeal powers, subdue his passions and appetites, and live upon the earth, as if he were not of the earth, enjoying the bounties of Providence with cheerful gratitude; doing good to his fellow men, and exalting, by rational dicipline, his own character, and the character of his race.— This is his greatest glory—this is his highest happiness—this is his obvious duty.

The faculties which thus constitute the high and distinguishing privilege of man, exalting him above all that surrounds him, and placing him but " a little lower than the angels," are progressive and improveable. It is true, also, that the bodily powers are capable of some improvement. But the measure of their growth is limited; and, comparatively, it is soon attained.— Their highest perfection seems to continue but for a moment. The intellectual and moral capacity, on the contrary, flourishes more and more with culture—becomes continually enlarged and invigorated, and yields a daily and increasing harvest, even when the bodily powers are visibly declining.

When the bloom has forsaken the cheek—when the beautiful smoothness of youth has yielded to the furrows of age, and the step has begun to lose something of its elasticity and briskness— the cultivated and disciplined mind, nourished by wholesome food, and enlivened by exercise, is still advancing in its career, extending the sphere of its beneficent influence, and, as it were, supplying, by its own graces, the ravages which time has made in the external form. The light within, if duly trimmed and fed, continues to spread its lustre with unabated, and even increasing splendour, when the frame that encloses it has lost its freshness, and begun to grow dim from age.

But we must also remember, that these faculties are liable to debasement and degeneracy. They will rust from sloth and indolence—they will decay from want of exercise and nourishment—and they will be smothered and destroyed, if subjected to the dominion of our passions and appetites. *That* is an empire they cannot endure. They were intended to be masters— and they will not submit to exist as slaves. The sluggard suffers the light of his intellect to go out. The drunkard drowns and extinguishes it. The one sinks into a state of calm brutality—the other, with frenzy in his brain, resembles more a savage and maddened animal rushing upon his own destruction, but dangerous to all who are in his way. Both are guilty in the same kind, though not in the same degree. They destroy the chief talent committed to man, and they degrade and dishonour his nature.

It has already been remarked, that the higher and nobler faculties of man will not exist in subjection to his sensual nature. They decline, decay and perish, unless they are allowed to exercise the authority allotted to them by a wise Providence. The moment their just empire is successfully invaded, they begin to languish—resistance becomes gradually more feeble, until at length they are overpowered and destroyed. And what then is the condition of the individual? Wisdom and virtue are synonymous, and happiness is their attendant reward. Folly and vice, on the contrary, not only lead to misery, but are sure to be accompanied by it at every step. In their first efforts to shake off the wholesome restraints of reason and conscience, they have to maintain a painful conflict with the accusers within, which constantly mars and disappoints their expected enjoyment. The poison is manifest in the cup, and they feel that it is there. They may throw off the *rein* of reason and conscience, but they will still suffer from the *lash!* When they have gained the victory, (as it must be admitted they may,) they have subverted the natural empire which Providence had intended should be established; and in the wild misrule which follows, the conquerors are sure to be the victims of the disorder and confusion they have created.

. Vicious indulgence destroys the body as well as the soul. It brings to an untimely end the very capacity for enjoyment. Its food is its deadly poison. Does the sluggard enjoy his sloth? It is impossible. *There is no rest without labour.* Unbroken idleness is more irksome than severe exertion; and it has no relief. The diligent man has delight in his honest occupation, even though it be wearisome; and he rejoices in the repose which he earns by it. He, and he alone, can duly estimate the force of the truth, that *the sabbath is made for man!* He is thankful for the refreshment and rest it affords him; while the habitual idler finds that it only increases his weariness. Has the drunkard or the debauchee any enjoyment? He has scarcely taken one step in the delirious path, before he begins to totter, and finds that by associating with vice, he has made a companion also of disease. They fasten upon him together; and however he may for a while be deluded, he soon becomes their conscious and degraded slave, the contempt of mankind gradually settling upon him, and his own reason approving the justness of their sentence. The base chains he wears are of his own forging. His own are the pain and the disgrace they inflict.

Self-denial and discipline are the foundation of all good character—the source of all true enjoyment—the means of all just distinction. This is the invariable law of our nature. Excellence of every sort is a prize, and a reward for virtuous, patient, and well directed exertion, and abstinence from whatever may encumber, enfeeble or delay us in our course. The approach to its lofty abode is rightly represented as steep and rugged.— He who would reach it must task his powers—But it is a noble task! for, besides the eminence it leads to, it nourishes a just ambition, subdues and casts off vicious propensities, and strengthens the powers employed in its service, so as to render them continually capable of higher and higher attainments.

What mean the cheers which greet the ingenuous youth, when he arrives at the high honours of a seminary of learning? Why do the hearts of his parents swell with unusual gladness, and tears burst forth to relieve their almost suffocating joy? Why is this epoch in life marked, as it every where is, with such intense and unabating interest? The race is not ended—it is only begun. One stage is reached, but another not less critical succeeds—and even when that is passed in safety, the whole way of life is beset with temptations and dangers, which require all our exertion, with the constant aid of a gracious Providence, to resist and avoid. Why, then I repeat, this heartfelt rejoicing? It is not merely that he has acquired the portion of learning which is taught in a College; though that is of inestimable value. It is that the youth, whose powers have thus been put forth and tried, has given a new earnest of character, and a new assurance of hope. His habits are measurably formed—his nobler faculties expanded—and his future elevation, in some degree indicated, by the strength of pinion displayed in his first flight.

As the mother's eye marks with inexpressible delight the first steps of her child, and her ear catches, with thrilling rapture, the music of his earliest efforts to utter articulate sound, imparting her joy to the whole household, and making as it were a family jubilee—so is the attainment of the honours of a College naturally and justly regarded with deep emotion. It fixes an important period in what may be termed the infancy of manhood, demonstrating the existence of a capacity for usefulness, and for further and higher honours. Happy are the youth who enjoy the opportunity of a liberal education—happier still are they who diligently and successfully improve it!

It is not the design of this discourse to speak of education in general—but only to make a few remarks upon what is denominated a *liberal education*—that system of instruction which is adopted in the higher seats of learning, and leads to learned honours. Institutions of this description are rapidly increasing in every quarter of our country. If the establishment of numerous seminaries of learning is to be regarded as an evidence of a corresponding increase of demand for liberal education, founded upon a proper knowledge of its nature, a just appreciation of its advantages, and a fixed determination to uphold and even to elevate its standard, this circumstance must afford the highest satisfaction to the scholar, the patriot, and the philanthropist. It will promote the cause of sound learning—it will advance the honour of our country, and it will increase the happiness of mankind. That such may be its effect, every one must ardently desire.

But it must be obvious at the same time, that these advantages are only to be gained by maintaining unimpaired, and in all its integrity, the true character of the higher seminaries of learning. It is not their object to teach the simpler elements of knowledge. These must be first acquired elsewhere, as an indispensable preliminary to admission. Nor do they profess, as a part of the Collegiate course, to qualify individuals for particular employments in life. This is a matter of subsequent acquisition, frequently not decided upon till after the College studies are ended.

The design of a College, as it has been well said, is "to lay the foundation of a superior education;" not to teach fully any particular art or science, but to discipline the intellectual powers, and to store the mind with such knowledge as may lead to further attainments, and be useful in any of the occupations or pursuits which are likely to be the lot of those who have the advantage of a Collegiate education. In a word, to place distinctly before the student the high objects to be aimed at—to teach him how they are to be attained—to stimulate him by worthy motives—and, after unfolding to him his own powers, and the mode of employing them, to send him forth with a generous and well directed ambition, and an instructed and disciplined mind, to follow out the course in which he has thus been trained.

Such a system, it must be evident, admits of no concession to individual views or inclinations. It works by general means, and for a general end. It proposes the same instruction for all; the same discipline; the same rewards; proceeding upon the assumed basis, that the plan thus adopted is in itself the best calculated to produce the desired general result.

In Sparta, the education of youth was a public concern. At an early age, children were taken from their parents, and placed under the care of masters appointed by the state, to prepare them, according to their notions, to become good citizens. The ancient Persians and the Cretans adopted a similar plan. With them too, education was a matter of public regulation. Among the Athenians and Romans, youth were not thus detached by law from the authority and care of their parents. But their education was justly deemed to be a matter of the highest importance, and conducted, no doubt, upon a general system, adapted to their manners and circumstances. Whatever opinion we may entertain of the methods they adopted, and the end they proposed—however different may have been the character intended to be formed, by the institutions of the Spartans and the Persians, from that which modern education proposes to cultivate—yet there is one point which has the sanction of their authority as well as the authority of succeeding times—that the education of youth having reference to a determined end, ought to be conducted upon a general plan, and that plan the best that is attain-

2

able for the end proposed, and carried to the highest perfection of which it is susceptible It is not meant to be contended, that in modern times, and in large communities, when there is so great an inequality in the condition of men, the highest education is, or ever can be within the reach of all, or even of a very considerable number. In our own country, favoured as it is by the bounty of Providence, with advantages such as no nation has ever before enjoyed, how many are there to whom the benefits even of the humblest education are not extended! Enlightened benevolence is happily exerting itself with unwearied diligence, to remedy this reproachful evil; and it is to be hoped that the time will soon come, when not a child will be left destitute of the means of acquiring at least the simpler elements of knowledge. This, however, is a subject of vast extent and interest, upon which it is not intended now to touch.

When, therefore, we speak of a " *superior education*," or a " *liberal education*," or, which ought to be equivalent, a " *collegiate education*," we speak of that which has one common purpose, or object, and which of course is necessarily itself but one. That it is applicable to all the youth of a country, whatever may be their condition or preparation, or whatever may be their future views in life, is what, as already intimated, it is not intended to affirm. The greater number cannot enjoy its advantages. At the age when the course of instruction in a College usually begins, some are obliged to labour for their subsistence; some are condemned to lasting ignorance by the neglect of parents or friends, or by the imperious force of circumstances; and some are already fixed to the occupations which are to employ their maturer years. We would not be understood by this remark to suggest, that superiority consists in the advantages we possess—it is only in the use we make of them, for which we are responsible, exactly in the proportion of their extent. All honest industry is honourable, as well as useful Nothing is disgraceful but idleness and vice; and the disgrace they bring with them is greater or less, as our opportunities have been more or less favourable. In the judgment of mankind, as well as in the awful judgment of Him from whom we have received all that we possess, the improvement required of us is according to the talent committed to our care. Much is therefore expected of him who has the means of attaining the highest intellectual and moral advancement. He is not to look down with a feeling of pride, upon other employments or conditions of life, as if they were inferior; but comparing himself with the most diligent in each—to examine whether he has equally with them improved the talents and opportunities vouchsafed to him—whether, in the race of honest exertion—the only generous competition that all can engage in—he has equalled, or excelled them—whether he has better or worse fulfilled the duty he owes to his day and generation.

The humblest labourer, who strenuously performs his daily task, and honestly provides an independent subsistence for himself and his family, is inconceivably superior to the sluggard and idler, though the latter may have had the opportunity of education in a seminary of learning.

There are some, who suppose that the business of instruction might be better adapted to the inclinations and views of individuals—that each student in a College might be taught only that which he desires to learn, and be at liberty to dispense with such branches of learning as appeared to him unnecessary or inapplicable, and yet receive Collegiate honours! This is an opinion which is perhaps gaining ground, and which, it cannot be denied, has been adopted by several distinguished men, and supported by plausible arguments.

Education, in all its parts, is a concern of so much consequence, so deeply and vitally interesting, that it ought not to be exposed, without great caution, to hazardous experiments and innovations. Is it, then, susceptible of no improvement? Is the human mind, progressive upon all other subjects, to be stationary upon this? Shall not education be allowed to advance with the march of intellect, and its path be illuminated with the increased and increasing light of the age? Or shall it be condemned to grope in the imperfect twilight, while every thing else enjoys the lustre of a meridian sun? These are imposing questions which are not to be answered by a single word. Admitting the general truth of that which they seem to assert, namely, that education, in all its departments, ought to be carried to the highest attainable perfection, and that the methods of reaching that point deserve our most anxious and continued attention—it must at the same time be apparent, that as long as the argument is merely speculative, implying objections to existing methods of instruction, and raising doubts about their value, without offering a distinct and approved substitute, great danger is to be apprehended from its circulation.

There is no doubt that improvement may be made in the seminaries of our country—there is no doubt that it ought to be made—and it is quite certain that it requires nothing but the support of enlightened public sentiment to bring it into operation. The improvement adverted to is improvement in degree—a better preparation for admission into College—a somewhat later age, and of course more mature powers—and, as a consequence, higher and more thorough teaching. The result can not be secured, unless the means are employed; and their employment does not depend upon those who are immediately entrusted with the care of the instruction of youth. Professors and teachers would unfeignedly rejoice in raising the standard of education—in advancing their pupils further and further in the path of learning—if parents, duly estimating its importance, could be prevailed upon to afford them the opportunity—for *they*, (unless totally unfit for their trust,) must be justly and conscientiously convinced of the value of such improvement. But their voice is scarcely listened to. By a prejudice, as absurd and unreasonable as it is unjust, *they* are supposed to be seeking only to advance their own interest; and *their* testimony is, on that account, disregarded; when, upon every principle by which human evidence ought to be tried, it is entitled to the highest respect. *Their* means of knowledge are greater than those of other men. They learn from daily experience—they learn from constant and anxious meditation—they learn from habitual occupation. It is theirs to watch with parental attention, and with more than parental intelligence, the expanding powers of the pupils committed to their charge. It is theirs to observe the influence of discipline and instruction in numerous instances, as it operates upon our nature—and it is theirs, too, with parental feeling to note the issues of their labours, in the lives of those who have been under their charge—to rejoice with becoming pride, when following an alumnus of the College with the eye of affectionate tenderness, they see him steadily pursuing a straight forward and elevated path, and becoming a good and an eminent man— and to mourn, with unaffected sorrow over those who have fallen by the way, disappointing the hopes of their parents and friends, turning to naught the counsels and cares that have been bestowed upon them, and inflicting pain and misery upon all who felt an interest in their welfare. *Experto crede*, is the maxim of the law; and it is no less the maxim of common sense. Why is it not to be applied to the case under consideration, as it is to all others which are to be determined by evidence? The sneering and vulgar insinuation sometimes hazarded by those who find it easier to sneer and insinuate, than to reason, that teachers, as a body, have a peculiar interest of their own, sufficient, upon questions which concern their vocation, to bring into doubt the integrity of their judgment, and thus to make them incompetent to be witnesses, if rightly considered, is not so much an insult to this useful and honourable, and I may add, in general, faithful class of men, as it is to the parents who entrust them with their children. What judgment shall we form of *their* intelligence—what shall we say of *their* regard for their offspring, if, at the most critical period of life, they place the forming intellect in the hands of men of more than questionable integrity, to be fashioned by them into fantastic shapes to suit their own purposes, or gratify their own whims? The truth is, that it is an appeal to ignorance, which can succeed only with those who are unable or unwilling to think, and is employed chiefly for want of solid argument.

The circumstances of our country, it must be admitted, have

encouraged and have favoured an early entrance into life, and so far have been averse to extended education. This cause has naturally, and to a certain extent justifiably, induced parents to yield to the restless eagerness of youth, always anxious to escape from the trammels of discipline, and confide in the strength of their untried powers.

Pride, too, a false and injurious pride is apt to lend its assistance. Instead of measuring the child's progress by his advancement in learning and in years, the parent is too much inclined to dwell only upon the advance he has made in his classes, and to note, with peculiar gratification, the fact, that he is the youngest of the graduates. Often, when it is evident to the teacher, that the pupil's lasting interest would be promoted by reviewing a part of his course, the very suggestion of being put back, is received as an affront, and indignantly rejected, though offered from the kindest and best considered motives. It is a mistake, a great mistake. To hurry a youth into College, and hurry him out of it, that he may have the barren triumph of extraordinary forwardness, is to forget the very end and object of education, which is to give him the full benefit of all that he can acquire in the period, which precedes his choice of a pursuit for life. What is gained by it? If, as frequently happens, he be too young to enter upon the study of a profession, there is an awkward interval when he is left to himself; he is almost sure to misapply and waste his precious time, and is in great danger of contracting permanent habits of idleness and dissipation. But even should this not be the case, of what consequence is it to him, that he should enter upon a profession a year sooner or later, compared with the loss of the opportunity of deepening, and widening and strengthening the foundations of character, which are then to be laid in a Seminary of learning. This opinion is not without decided support. Many intelligent parents have been observed to adopt it in practice, voluntarily lengthening out the education of their children beyond the ordinary limits. Such an improvement as has now been alluded to, ought unquestionably to be aimed at. The progress of liberal education ought to bear some proportion to the rapid advances our country is making in other respects, and to the character and standing which her wealth, her strength, and her resources require her to maintain. It is especially due to the nature of our Republican institutions, in order to win for them still higher esteem with mankind, that their capacity should be demonstrated, to encourage and produce whatever is calculated to adorn and to improve our nature, and to contribute our full proportion to the great society of learning and letters in the world. It would be much to be regretted, if the multiplication of colleges were to have the contrary effect, of lowering the standard of education, or of preventing its progressive elevation. Let the competition among them be, not who shall have the most pupils within their walls, but who shall make the best scholars!

But may there not be improvement in kind, as well as in degree? May not the course of studies itself be beneficially altered, excluding some, which are now in use, and adopting others which have not hitherto been introduced—changing the relative importance of different objects of study—making those secondary, which at present are principal, and those principal which are now, in some degree, secondary—or, adopting a flexible and yielding system, may not the studies be accommodated to the views and wishes of individuals, permitting each pupil to pursue those, and those only, which he or his parents or friends may think proper to select as best adapted to his expected plan of life? It would be rash and presumptuous to answer that such improvement is impossible; and it would be unwise, if it were practicable, to check or discourage the investigation of matters so important to the welfare of man. The subject is one which at all times deserves the most careful consideration; and the highest intellect cannot be better employed than in examining it in all its bearings. But its unspeakable importance inculcates also the necessity of great caution. It is dangerous to unsettle foundations. Doubts and objections to existing systems, without a plain and adequate substitute, are calculated only to do mischief. By bringing into question the value of present methods of instruction, they tend to weaken public confidence, to paralyze the efforts of the teacher, and to destroy or enfeeble the exertions of the student. A strong conviction of the excellence of the end, is the indispensable incitement to the toil of attaining it. Without this stimulus, in all its vigour, nothing rational will be achieved. The love of ease, which is natural to us all, will lend a ready ear to the suggestion, that labour would be wasted; and the misguided youth, doubting the usefulness of the task that is before him, and expecting something (he knows not what) more worthy of his zeal and energy, will be like the foolish man, who stood upon the bank of a river, waiting for the water to run out, and leave the channel dry for him to pass over.

Experimentum in corpore vili, is the cautious maxim of physics. A generation of youth is of too great value to be experimented upon; and education is of too much consequence to hazard its loss, by waiting for the possible discovery of better methods. It is a great public concern, and should be dealt with accordingly, until a specific change shall be proposed, which, upon a deliberate and careful examination, shall meet the acceptance of the greater part of those who are best able to judge, so that they can conscientiously, and with full conviction, recommend it to general adoption, as entirely worthy of public confidence, let us cling to that which has been proved to be good. Quackery is odious in all things, but in none more than in this. *Stare super vias antiquas*, is a safe precept for all, at least until a way be pointed out that is clearly and demonstrably better.

Speculation, however ingenious, is not knowledge; nor are doubts and objections to be entertained, where decision is of such vital importance. Time is rushing on—Youth is passing away. The moments, that are gliding by us, will never return. The seed time neglected, there will be no good harvest. Poisonous and hateful weeds may occupy the soil, which, under good culture, would have yielded excellent fruit. The craving appetite of youth must be satisfied. If not supplied with sound and wholesome food, it will languish for want of sustenance, or perhaps drink in poison and destruction. The brute animal, without reason, is guided by an unerring direction, to the provision made for its support, each individual obeying his own instinct, without aid or counsel or restraint from the others. But man, excepting the direction he receives to the beautiful fountain of nourishment, provided for the short period of helpless and unconscious infancy, has no such determining instinct. He has a large range, and a free choice. "The world is all before him, where to choose;" and reason is given, to select for him that which is for his advantage. Nor is the rational individual left dependent upon his own unassisted intelligence for his guidance. Until his faculties, which are progressive, have arrived at a certain maturity, it is in the order of Providence, that he should have the benefit of the enlightened reason of his species imparted to him, for his own sake, by parents, by teachers, by friends, and by the counsels of the wise and the virtuous, which he cannot enjoy but upon the terms of being subjected to their authority. It is theirs to lead him on his way—it is his to follow the path they point to. But if the guide stand doubting and perplexed, what will become of the follower?

That a Collegiate education can be so modified as that each student may be permitted to choose his own studies generally, or even to a limited extent, and yet receive the honours of a College, is a proposition, which, to say the least of it, must be deemed to be very questionable.

Without intending to occupy your time with any thing like a discussion of this question, it may, nevertheless, be allowable to remark, that the suggestion, however plausible in itself, seems to be founded in an erroneous conception of the nature of such an education. However it may be styled a Collegiate education—a superior education—a liberal education—it is still only a portion of preliminary education. It is not designed, as has already been stated, to qualify the student in a special manner for any particular profession or pursuit—to make him a Divine, or a Lawyer, or a Physician—but to aid in the developement of all his faculties in their just proportions; and by discipline and

3

instruction, to furnish him with those general qualifications, which are useful and ornamental in every profession, which are essential to the successful pursuit of letters in any of their varied forms, and, if possible, even more indispensible to the security and honour of a life of leisure. Nor does it set up the extravagant pretention of supplying him with a stock of knowledge sufficient for all purposes, and sufficient for its own preservation, without further exertion. It gives him the keys of knowledge, and instructs him how to use them for drawing from the mass, and adding to his stores. It teaches him the first and greatest of lessons—it teaches him how to learn, and inspires him at the same time, if it succeed at all, with that love of learning, which will invigorate his resolution in the continual improvement of this lesson. The momentum, if rightly communicated, and rightly received, will continue to be felt throughout his life. But it is unnecessary to dwell longer on this part of the subject, as it has lately received an ample and able exposition, in a report made by the Faculty of a neighbouring institution,* which, (if I may be permitted to venture a judgment upon the work of so learned a body,) does them the highest honour.

The suggestion under consideration would perhaps be entitled to more respect, if in fact the destination of youth for life always, or even generally, preceded their entrance into College. But that, it is believed, is not the case. The fond partiality of a parent may sometimes discern, or fancy it discerns in a child, the promise of eminence in some peculiar walk. But it would be unwise to decide finally, before a decision is necessary, and before the subject is ripe for decision. It is in the college that the youth has the last trial with his equals. There his growing powers are more fully exhibited, and placed in a clearer light. And there, too, it often happens, that an inclination is disclosed, which not being unreasonable in itself, a prudent and affectionate parent may think fit to indulge. The time of leaving College would, therefore, seem to be a much more suitable occasion for decision than

---

* Yale College.

the time of entering it. But even such a decision is not always unchangeable. How many instances have occurred, of youth, who, after receiving the benefits of a liberal education, have engaged in one pursuit, and subsequently, with the approbation of their parents and friends, have betaken themselves to another, with distinguished success! Several present themselves to my recollection, and some of them of men who have attained, and are now enjoying the highest eminence.

How often does it happen, much later in life, that men are compelled by circumstances, or constrained by a sense of duty, to change their occupations? It is precisely in such instances that the advantages of a liberal education are most sensibly felt— of that early training, and general preparation, which, not being exclusively intended for any one pursuit, are adapted to many, if not to all, and confer upon the individual a sort of universality of application and power. In a moment like this, the means which education has supplied come to our aid, like the neglected and almost forgotten gift of an old friend, hallowed and endeared by the associations they bring with them. And in such a moment, the individual who, has not had the same opportunity, most keenly feels the loss.

Nor must we forget that in this our country, every individual may be called upon to take a part in public affairs, and there to maintain his own character, and the character of the state or nation. And even should not this occur, still he is to mingle in the intercourse of polished society, where his station in the esteem and respect of others, will be assigned to him, according to the measure of his improvement and worth, estimated by the scale of his opportunities. Being, as it were, a part of the Corinthian capital of society, he will be unworthy of his place, if he is destitute of the ornaments and graces that belong to his station.

But upon the plan that is now in question, who is to choose for the youth the studies he will pursue? Surely it cannot be gravely asserted, that, at the usual age of entering into College, the choice ought to be left to himself. Why has Providence committed the care of children to the affectionate intelligence of parents? Why have human laws provided for them tutors and guardians? Why have schools, and seminaries of learning been established, and courses of education and discipline prescribed, but to give them the benefit of that experience and knowledge which they do not themselves possess?

To suppose that a youth, at such an age, is competent to decide for himself what he will learn, and how much he will learn, is to suppose that he has already had the experience of manhood, under the most favourable circumstances—that he is competent to educate himself—nay, that he is already educated—and instead of needing instruction, is qualified to impart it to others. Is the choice then to be made by parents? To them it undoubtedly belongs, as a right, to determine for their children, whether they will send them to College or not—but there their authority terminates. It cannot be pretended that every parent, or that any parent has, or ought to have, or can have a right to decide upon the discipline and instruction to be adopted in a College, though he has the power of withdrawing his child, if he think fit to do so.

Admitting parents to be fully competent to resolve a question of so much depth and difficulty—as many unquestionably are—and admitting, too, that their views are more wise and accurate, and entitled to greater deference than the collected and continued wisdom which has devised, and which preserves the system in being, still it would be obviously impracticable to indulge them. There could not, in such a case, be statutes, or laws, or discipline, or system. In short, there could be no government. To some, it may seem harsh, but it is believed to be perfectly true, that when a youth is once placed in a College, selected after due deliberation, the less interference there is on the part of the parent, except in cases of manifest wrong done to him, (which rarely or ever occur in our principal institutions,) and the more unreservedly the pupil is committed to the authorities of the institution, the better it will be both for parent and child.

Above all things, a parent should sedulously guard against the introduction of a doubt into the mind of a student, of the justice and necessity of the authority exercised over him, or of the excellence of the studies he is required to pursue. Such doubts must inevitably produce insubordination and indolence, and will end in the disappointment of his hopes. Enthusiastic and ardent zeal, an estimate even exaggerated, of the excellence of a given pursuit, amounting almost to folly in the judgment of bystanders, are the needful stimulants to successful enterprize.— Nothing great is achieved without them. The heart must go along with the understanding. A strong passion must take possession of the soul, inspiring it with warmth, and with enduring energy, and unconquerable resolution; so that all its faculties may be fully and steadily exerted, and overcoming the vis inertiæ of our nature, and deaf and blind to the temptations that would seduce it from its course, it may press forwards continually towards the prize which is to be the reward of its toils. Such ought to be the feelings of the youth who is favoured with the opportunity of a liberal education. Devotion to his studies, as excellent in themselves, affectionate respect for his teachers, as faithful guides and impartial judges, an honourable competition with his equals, in virtuous exertion, and a conscientious observance of the laws of the institution—these are the habits which will lay a deep foundation for the structure of future usefulness and eminence. The honours of the College, their first fruits, and their just reward, are the gratifying proofs of a capacity for further triumphs, and constitute the richest, and most acceptable offering which filial duty can present as an acknowledgement and requital of parental care.

That part of a course of liberal education, however, which has been most frequently assailed, is the study of the Greek and Roman Classics—what is emphatically called Classical learning. Some have insisted that it ought to be altogether excluded; and others, that it does not deserve to occupy so much of the time and attention of youth. Mr. LOCKE, who himself enjoyed the full benefit of the treasures of ancient learning, seems to make a compromise of the matter; for while he admits that the languages may be useful to those who are designed for the learned professions, or for the life of a gentleman without a profession, he seems to consider that they, as well as philosophy, are calculated rather to have an injurious effect upon the general character, than otherwise. The broader ground of entire exclusion, however, as has already been said, has had its advocates. Many years ago, a distinguished citizen of the United States, whose memory, let it be said, is entitled to great veneration, among other things for the example he gave of untiring industry and youthful vigour in his varied pursuits, continued to almost the last day of a long life, published an Essay, in which, with his usual ingenuity and force, he contested the value of Classical learning as a branch of education. It appears from a subsequent publication, by the same author, that this Essay produced many replies, and that it also produced a complimentary letter (now published with the Essay,) from a gentleman who is stated to have been at that time the Principal of an academy. In this letter, after complimenting the author, the writer proceeds as follows—" There is little taste for them (the learned languages,) in this place. In our academy, where there are near ninety students, not above nineteen are poring over Latin and Greek. One of these nineteen was lately address-ed by a student of Arithmetic in the following language—' Pray, sir, can you resolve me, by your Latin, this question? If one bushel of corn cost four shillings, what cost fifty bushels?' A demand of this kind, from a youth, is to me a proof of the taste of Americans in the present day, who prefer the *useful* to the *ornamental!*" This was surely an extraordinary triumph over the poor Latinist, and a very singular evidence of what the good Principal was pleased to call " American taste!" Who ever im-agined that the study of the Greek and Latin would teach a boy the first rules of Arithmetic? Or who was ever absurd enough to contend that Greek and Latin were to be taught to the exclusion of the simplest elements of pure Mathematics? They have their appropriate uses and advantages; but they do not profess to be themselves the whole of education, nor to accom-plish every thing that is desirable. They do not give sight to the blind, nor hearing to the deaf, nor speech to the dumb; but when these faculties exist in their usual perfection—as is happily the case with the far greater part of mankind—and there is the ordinary portion of talent, they furnish an occupation, which is both useful and ornamental, which is not inconsistent with the necessary attainments in mathematics, and which may not only well go along with the acquisition of our own language, but is deemed to be indispensable to its accurate knowledge, and highest enjoyment.

But however feeble was the commentary of the Principal, and however ignorant was the argument of the "student of arithmetic," yet, for him, it was not in a wrong spirit. Arithmetic was his pursuit, and it was fit that he should think well of it.— But the poor student of Latin! What could be expected from *his* labours in a Seminary where the study was systematically depreciated; and the head of it, from whom he was to look for encouragement and assistance, gloried (conscientiously, no doubt,) in having nearly expelled it from his school? The teacher might, and probably did endeavour to perform his duty; but it must have been coldly and heartlessly done. Instead of breathing warmth and animation into the atmosphere, to invigorate the tender plants entrusted to his care, they must have been in imminent danger of being stunted in their growth, by chilling and withering indifference.

Of the opinions which have been mentioned, the one proposing entirely to exclude the ancient languages from a course of liberal instruction—and the other, to reduce the time and attention devoted to them, it would be difficult to say, that as applied to this country, the one is more to be deprecated than the other. Are the languages overtaught now? Will they bear a reduction? The reverse is known to be the fact. Compared with the teaching in the German schools, where the design is to make scholars, compared with the teaching in the schools of England, where the design, in addition to this, is to qualify men for all the higher employments of life, as well as for a life without particular employment, it can scarcely be said that here they are taught at all. Excepting in the profession of divinity, is it too strong to affirm that there is scarcely such a thing as scholarship? And even in that profession, how many are there, in proportion to the whole number engaged in its sacred duties, who would be able to encounter a learned Infidel with the weapons of ancient learning? We have eminent lawyers—we have distinguished physicians—enterprising and intelligent merchants—and a fund of general talent capable of the highest elevation in every employment or pursuit of life. Occasionally we meet with one among them, commonly of the old stock, in whom are discerned the elegant influences of Classical literature.

But where are our eminent scholars? Where are the greater lights, ruling with a steady and diffusive splendour, and vindicating their claim to a place among the constellations which shine in the firmament of learning? Nay, how few are there among us, of our best educated men, who, if called upon to bring forth their stores, would be able to say with Queen Elizabeth, that they had "brushed up their Latin," or would have any Latin to brush up? The truth is that this branch of study is already at the very minimum, if not below it. It will not bear the least reduction. It positively requires to be increased in teaching, and raised in public esteem. Classical learning neither falls in showers, nor flows in streams. Here and there a solitary drop appears, sparkling and beautiful to be sure, like the last dew on a leaf, but too feeble, without the support of its kindred element, even to preserve itself, and utterly powerless to enrich or fructify the neighbouring soil. To propose a reduction, is therefore equivalent, at least, to an entire exclusion, if it be not worse. Less taught than it now is, or less esteemed, the teaching would be almost a false pretence, and the learning a waste of time. It would be as well at once to blot it from the course, and, as far as in our power lies, to let the Greek and Latin languages sink into oblivion, and be lost in profound darkness, like that from which, by their single power, they have once recovered the world.

This would be a parricidal work for civilization and science. But if it is to be accomplished, the mode is not what is to characterize it as unnatural. Before we advance to a conclusion of such incalculable importance, let us first consider what it is, and then endeavour to be fully assured that it is right. If it be once decided that the study of the ancient languages can be dispensed with in a Collegiate education, and the honours of a College obtained without it, there is no difficulty in perceiving it must also be dropped in the preparatory schools. Why begin it, if it is not to be pursued? Why take up time in acquiring what is afterwards to be thrown aside as rubbish, and forgotten? Forgotten it inevitably will be, if it be entirely discontinued at the time of entering College, By what motives or arguments will a boy be persuaded to apply himself to learning in a Grammar School, what is not necessary to obtain for him the honours of a College, and what he is distinctly told will be of no use to him in life? It is absurd to think of it. The youngest child has sagacity enough to understand an argument, which coincides with his own inclination, and to apply it to the indulgence of his own natural love of ease. Tell him that he might as well be unemployed, and, without having ever studied logic, he will be very apt to jump at once to the seductive conclusion of idleness.

These languages, let it be remembered, have hitherto not merely formed a part, they have been the very basis of a liberal education. I might almost say they have been education itself. From the revival of letters to the present time, they have held this station, through a period of five hundred years, not in one country only, but in all the civilized world. They gained it by their own merits, and they have kept it by their unquestionable success. Would it be wise or prudent to cast them off, unless we were fully prepared to supply the large space they have occupied, by something equal, at least, if not superior? This is no metaphysical question; nor does the answer to it require the peculiar powers of Mr. LOCKE, mighty as they confessedly were.— It is eminently a practical question, which common sense is fully able to decide. It may be stated thus; Education, having a given end, and a certain plan of education, having approved itself during some hundreds of years, and still continuing daily to approve itself to be well suited to attain that end, is it wise or

4

rational to require that it shall be vindicated upon original
grounds, and be rejected like a novelty, unless it can be justifi-
ed to our complete satisfaction, by arguments *a priori?* That
is a good time-keeper which keeps good time, no matter how
constructed. That is good food which is found to nourish the
body, whatever peptic precepts may say to the contrary. And
that is good exercise, which gives vigour and grace to the limbs,
even though a Chinese lady might not be allowed to use it.—
Against such a fact, once well established, argumentative objection ought to be unavailing, or there is an end to all just reasoning.

> "What can we reason, but from what we know?"

This proof is manifest, in respect to nations, as it is in respect
to individuals. It is astonishing, that Mr. Locke could have entertained the suggestion for a moment, that the study of the
languages and philosophy was unfriendly to the formation of
prudent and strong character, when he looked around upon his
countrymen, and perceived, as he must have done, that they are
not less distinguished for their attachment to these studies, than
for what Mr. Burke has called "the family of grave and mas-
culine virtues." Constancy, resolution, unconquerable spirit, a
lofty determination never under any circumstances of adversity
to admit the betraying counsels of fear, were not more signally
exhibited by the old Romans, when Hannibal, triumphant, and
seemingly irresistible, from the slaughter at Cannæ, was thun-
dering at the gates of Rome, than they have been by that nation,
which Mr. Locke's genius has contributed to illustrate and
adorn. This same study has gone hand in hand with every
profession and pursuit, refining, exalting and dignifying them
all. Theologians, statesmen, lawyers, physicians, poets, orators, philosophers, the votaries of science and of letters, have
been disciplined and nourished by it, and under the influence of
its culture have attained the highest excellence. The arts of
life have, at the same time, kept on with steady pace, so that the
people whom Cesar spoke of as, in his time, "*Britannos toto
orbe divisos,*" now, if not in all respects at the very head of the

European family, are certainly not inferior to any of its members. Let those who cavil at a liberal education, and those especially who question the value of the Greek and Latin languages, answer this fact. The tree cannot be bad which produces such fruit. It is unphilosophical to doubt the adequacy of a cause to produce a given effect, when we see that the effect is constantly produced by that cause ; and it is unphilosophical to search for another cause, when we have found one that is sufficient. If the study of the ancient languages has been found, by long experience, to discipline and nourish the intellectual faculties, why should we doubt that it is efficacious for that purpose? Why should we go about to seek for something else, that if it succeed will but answer the same purpose—and if it fail, leaves us entirely destitute? One will flippantly tell us that it is spending too much time about words, which could be better employed about things. The great British lexicographer has unintentionally given some countenance to this notion, in the Preface to his Dictionary. A man, who had accomplished such a labour, might be permitted, at its close, to feel the departure of the spirit which had sustained him in its progress, and in the pathetic melancholy of taking leave, so eloquently expressed as almost to draw tears from the reader, he might be allowed even to depreciate his own work, by admitting that "words are the daughters of earth, and that things are the sons of heaven." But even the authority of Dr. Johnson cannot be permitted thus to degrade the pedigree of words, or diminish their importance. Articulate sound is from heaven. Its origin is divine. The faculty of speech is the immediate gift of Him who made us, and its destitution (which his good Providence sometimes allows to occur) is felt to be a great calamity. Language—words—are the exercise of this faculty, as thought is the exercise of the faculty of thinking. The one is worthy of improvement, as well as the other—nay, we can scarcely conceive of their separate existence, or their separate cultivation—and hence the first step in the instruction of the dumb is to teach them the use of language. Words without thought are idle and vain. Thought, without the

power of expressing it, is barren and unproductive. "Proper
words in proper places," is the point we all strive to attain; and
this is what constitutes the perfection of the power of commu-
nicating with each other. Is is true, therefore, that "words are
things;" and there is no better proof of it than this, that the
most extraordinary, may I not say the most vulgar error sometimes obtains currency, by means of an epigrammatick sentence,
by the mere charm of the collocation of words. The fact is,
that they occupy our attention throughout our lives; and a
greater or less command of them is one of the chief visible
distinctions that mark the different orders of intelligence. The
child is taught to speak, to spell, and to read—the youth to declaim and to compose—and the *man* strives perpetually to improve
and perfect himself in the use of language, by frequent exercise,
and the study of the best models. Demosthenes is said to have
copied the history of Thucydides eight times with his own hand,
and to have committed the greater part of it to memory, merely
to improve his style. His orations were composed with the ut-
most care; and they were retouched, improved, and corrected
with the minuteness of a Flemish painter—even to the altera-
tion of parts of words. He was never satisfied till he had given
the highest possible finish to his work. Was this an idle labour?
More than two thousand years have since rolled by; and the
language of Athens, in the days of Demosthenes, cannot be
said to be now spoken in the world. Yet is he confessed to be
the undisputed master in his noble art. His orations, said by
a strong figure to have been as an earthquake in ancient Greece,
still agitate the bosom which is sensible of the powers of eloquence, and offer the best model to its votaries. Like the fine
remains of the Grecian chisel, they stand in severe, but beautiful and commanding simplicity, as if conscious that their title to
respect, being founded in nature and in truth, though perfected
by consummate skill, was equally available in every age.*

---

* Cicero not only studied the Greek language, but to such an extent as to be
able to declaim in it, and to excite the strong but melancholy admiration of Appo-
lonius. "As for you, Cicero," he said, after hearing him declaim in Greek, "I

If it therefore be conceded that the study of the ancient languages is calculated to assist us in what is disparagingly termed the learning of words, or, as it ought to be expressed, in acquiring a good style—that it improves the taste, and corrects the judgment—this, though but a part of its merits, would go far to vindicate its right to a place in every system of liberal education.

Sometimes it is objected, as it was by the Principal of an academy, already quoted, that an acquaintance with these languages is ' ornamental,' but not ' useful.' The meaning of this objection depends upon two words, which, appearing to be exact, are notwithstanding, as ambiguous, perhaps, as any in our vocabulary. They are often used without a definite sense in the mind of the speaker, and very seldom with any certainty of the same understanding on the part of the hearer. If it were necessary to endeavour to be precise on this subject, we might be permitted to say, that in the opinion of many very intelligent people, nothing is properly ornamental that is not in some way useful. But when we have thus disentangled ourselves of one perplexing word, we are obliged to encounter another. What is useful, and what is not useful? Are mankind agreed about it? By no means. How then are we to determine what is useful? The answer seems to be this—we are to arrive at a conclusion by considering man in his various relations, and thence inferring, as we justly may, that every thing is useful which contributes to the improvement or the innocent gratification of himself or of others, or qualifies him more effectually or acceptably to perform his duties. Does any one object to those exercises of youth, which give a graceful carriage to the body? Are they not admitted to be useful? And is it less important to give a graceful carriage to the mind? Are good manners, the external graces, worthy to be cultivated, because they give pleasure to others? And are the graces of the intellect to be entirely neglected? Is the generous youth to be told that nothing is necessary but to be able to compute the cost

praise and admire you: but I am concerned for the fate of Greece. She had nothing left her but the glory of eloquence and education, and you are carrying that too to Rome."

of fifty bushels of corn? The proprieties, and even the ele-
gancies of life, when they do not run away with the heart, nor
interfere with the performance of serious duties, are well deserv-
ing our attention.   But let it not be imagined, that in thus insis-
ting upon the general argument of experience—the greatest of
all teachers—in favour of Classical learning, or in answering
one or two particular objections, it is meant to be conceded,
that it cannot be vindicated upon original grounds.   It can be,
and it has been, repeatedly and triumphantly shown, that these
unequalled languages, which, as was long ago said of them,
"have put off flesh and blood, and become immutable," are precisely calculated to perform the most important general offices
of a liberal education, in a manner that no other known study
will accomplish.   They awaken attention—they develope and
employ the reasoning faculty—they cultivate the taste—they
nourish the seeds of the imagination—give employment to the
memory—and, in a word, they discipline and invigorate, in due
proportion, all the intellectual powers, and prepare them for or-
derly and effective exertion in all the varied exigencies which
may require their action.   Nor is this all.   They lay the foundation of that learning which will abide with us, and increase
our enjoyments in all the vicissitudes of life.

   But the limits of a discourse would be unreasonably transcen-
ded, by an attempt to enter into a more particular examination
of this part of the subject.   Nor is it necessary that I should
thus trespass upon your patience, already so largely taxed —
Abler heads, and stronger hands—strong in good learning—
have been repeatedly employed upon the work—and I should
only enfeeble their demonstration, by attempting to restate the
process.   As a witness, however, stating the result of his observations, confirmed by the observations of others, I may be
allowed to say, that to a young man, entering upon the study of a
liberal profession, a thorough groundwork of Classical education is like a power gained in mechanics, or rather it is the foundation wanted by Archimedes for his fulcrum!   It gives him a
mastery of his studies which nothing else can supply.   Of its

other influences, allow me to quote to you the testimony of a distinguished female, who, to uncommon opportunities united extraordinary genius and power of observation, and is entirely free from all suspicion of partiality. "The English Universities, (says Madame de Stael, in her 'Germany,') have singularty contributed to diffuse among the people of England that knowledge of ancient languages and literature, which gives to their orators and statesmen an information so liberal and brilliant. It is a mark of good taste to be acquainted with other things besides matters of business, *when one is thoroughly acquainted with them;* and, besides, the eloquence of free nations attaches itself to the history of the Greeks and Romans, as to that of ancient fellow countrymen. * * * * The study of languages, which forms the basis of instruction in Germany, is much more favourable to the progress of the faculties in infancy, than that of the Mathematics and Physical sciences." For this she quotes the admission of Pascal.

Some part of the doubt, which, in this country, has been insinuating itself into the public mind, is owing to the imperfect and insufficient manner in which the languages have been taught; or rather it should be said, in which they have been learned; for there has probably been at all times a disposition to teach them. Enough has not been acquired to fix a permanent taste in the student himself, or to demonstrate its value to others. The consequence is, that the graduate suffers his little stock to decay from neglect, and his parents and friends exclaim that learning is of no use. Another consequence is, that there is no scholar-like mind, to exert its influence upon the community, and operate upon the mass of public opinion. The corrective is in more thorough teaching. It will require more time and more labour from the student. But time thus employed, will be well employed. And as to labour—if he desire to arrive at excellence of any sort, he can learn nothing better than how to apply himself with diligence to the work that is before him. There is a great deal of affectation in the world, of facility and expedition in the performance of intellectual tasks—of doing things quickly, and without preparation or exertion, as if by an inspiration of genius, and differently from those, who, by way of derision, are called plodders! It is a poor affectation. Sometimes it is maintained at the expense of sincerity, by concealing the pains that are really taken. Oftener it is only the blustering of conscious weakness and indolence. The highest and surest talent—that which will hold out longest, and often reach the greatest elevation—the only talent, I might almost say, which is given to man for intellectual achievement—is the talent of applying his faculties to produce a good result—that is, of labouring with success. No one need be ashamed of possessing, of exercising, or of cultivating it. The great lesson of life is to apply ourselves diligently to what is before us. Life itself is but a succession of moments. The largest affairs are made up of small parts.— The greatest reputation is but the accumulation of successive fruits, each carefully gathered and stored. The most learned scholar began with learning words. Every day is by itself a day of small things. But the sum of our days, makes up our life—and the sum of our days' work makes up the work of our life. Let every one, therefore, who would arrive at distinction, remember, that the present moment is the one he is to improve, and apply himself diligently to its improvement.

.

CPSIA information can be obtained
at www.ICGtesting.com
Printed in the USA
BVHW041038170119
538075BV00017B/755/P